Business Opportunities Guide

Best Ideas For This Year

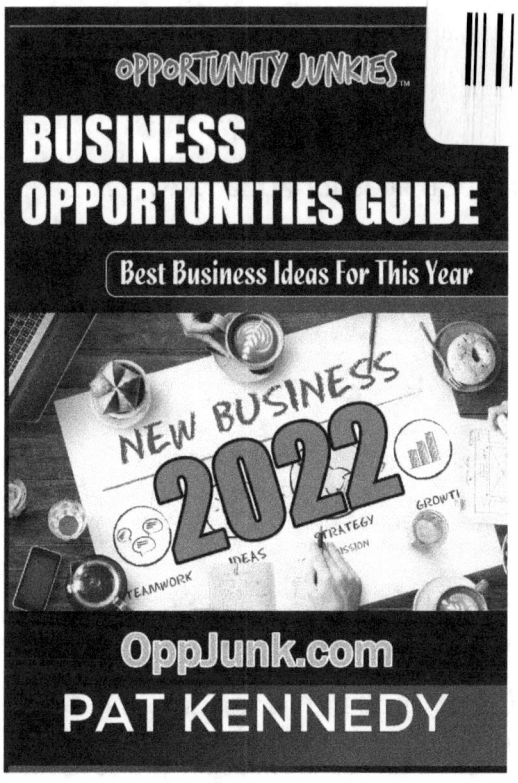

Copyright 2022

Table Of Content

Who This Book Is For

Someone who is undecided which business they would like to start in 2022, and doesn't have a lot of money to invest. Most of the businesses in this book require an investment of only $500 or less, with good to great income potential.

IMPORTANT NOTE - This is a business idea book. I do not get into the exact details on how to start, promote, and run each business.

The business idea listings in this book include a general overview of each business, current and future markets, earning potential, pros & cons, and a handful of helpful tips. This will not only help you decide which business you should start, but which ones might be a waste of time for you. Why waste a year on something that's not going to work out for you?

Note - I suggest you read most of the business ideas, even if you don't think they fit you. Sometimes they contain business principles or stories that pertain to *any* business.

The Opportunity Junkies Series

The Opportunity Junkies Series is for someone who is addicted to taking on new opportunities and challenges in life.

Written by a collection of authors with years of experience in many fields, it's all about passing on these experiences (both good and bad), so we can all learn from each other and better ourselves.

Whether you read the books, listen to the audio books, or visit the website OppJunk.com, we all thank you for your continued support.

About The Author

Hello my name is Pat Kennedy. I'm an entrepreneur who has run dozens of successful businesses since 1996. I've learned a *lot* during this time and have decided to become a part of the Opportunity Junkies series, so I can share my stories of business successes and failures.

And sometimes I'll throw in a funny story, just to break up the business professional monotony.

I'm also a Christian man. If Jesus or the Bible says it, that is what I believe. Those are my moral standards. If I were to eliminate this fact from all of my books, you wouldn't be getting the full picture. Note - You *can* make a lot of money being honest and fair in all of your business dealings. If lying, cheating, and stealing is part of the business plan, I'm out.

I've read many books that included amazing *quotes* from Steve Jobs, Bill Gates, David Goggins (a believer in God), Eric Thomas (a Christian man), Tony Robbins, etc. Well, in my books you might read a few quotes from Jesus Christ or his Bible. Jesus was on this earth just like the others. His words greatly helped me in my businesses and in life, and need to be included in my works. The NIV translation will always be used.

I'm only mentioning this because, regardless of your religious beliefs, everyone can learn from my life experiences.

Being successful at *anything* requires *faith*. Even if you don't believe in God, you *still* have to have faith in *some thing* (or someone). If you don't have faith that you'll eventually succeed, you'll never even try. Or you'll refuse to do what it takes to make it happen.

My faith is in God. I believe that through well thought out decisions, very hard work and prayer, *He* will bless our efforts. And He will...

"Truly I tell you, if you have faith as small as a mustard seed, you can say to this mountain, 'Move from here to there,' and it will move. Nothing will be impossible for you." (Matthew 17:20

My 5 Main Business Laws

Here are a few *must* business laws that I had to include in this book. Many are common sense, but *most* people starting a business disregard a few of them, and their businesses paid *dearly* for it.

1. You MUST MARKET Your Business, Products, Services
This is #1, and BY FAR #1. I know many business owners who got *only* this *one thing* right and made millions! Actually, this happens very often with many companies.

I know *so many* people who wrote a book, recorded a CD, wanted to be a blogger or youtuber, etc.and did ZERO promotion. Or they made a weak effort with social media, adding under 100 subscribers. *Everyone* I know who did this with their business made next to nothing, or they *lost* money. It's *impossible* to succeed if no one knows what you have to offer.

If you're someone who *refuses* to promote your business in some effective way, DON'T EVEN GET STARTED. With no marketing, your business success rate is so low, you might as well just play the lottery and save the time.

Now, I'm not saying *if* you market your business are *guaranteed* to make a lot of money. There are many factors that go into that. What I *am* saying is, if you do ZERO marketing you are *guaranteed* to FAIL.

2. You Must Put The Time In

I would have to say this is BY FAR #2. But then again, this partially ties into marketing. If you *refuse* to spend time and work with your business, it *will* fail.

This is common sense, or is it? I've worked with over a hundred clients and at least 75% outright *refused* to do *anything* with the business they wanted to start. Most of them wanted a passive income turnkey website. "Here's $500, just make me a website and I want $1k to go into my bank account at the end of every week. I don't want to do anything." **Everyone in the entire world wants this!!**

If anyone *could* make this free-money website, why would they waste their time and run a service business for other people? They would just make 1,000 of these websites for themselves and collect millions, while doing nothing!

This is the same as the guys on YouTube asking for $1,000 to tell you how to make $10k a month while doing nothing. *Why* are they selling you this "valuable" secret? Why don't they just apply their own secret using 1,000 different accounts and make $10 million a month? No, they'd rather sell this secret to you for a measly $1k and lose out a millions. Lol! Silly. Then they show a statement with all these bank deposits. Yes, they're real sales. Look closely, that's your $1,000 in there along with everyone else! That's not the money from actually *using* their own secret, it's from *selling* the secret to you.

I always explain to my clients the work that's required to make their business idea a success.

One guy tells me, "I just want to sit on the beach with my laptop and make $2k a week. And I don't want to have to do anything." I actually know several people who *do just that* ($2k a week from the beach). It is *possible.* But they worked 60 hours a week for several years to put themselves in this position, and the first few years they made very little income.

Another client tells me, once 3pm comes, the rest of the day is his time. But, he does have 2 hours a day he can squeeze in, to work on his business idea. " Wow, you have a whole 14 hours a week to put into your business…"

I asked him what he did after 3pm? He said, "Watch TV, eat, bowl, golf, etc." Building a successful business was NOT a big priority in his life. Nor did he ever achieve it.

Like I mentioned earlier, 75% of the people I've worked with give me some variation of one of the stories above. "I want to do nothing, and become rich." It doesn't work that way for anyone.

No one has ever said to me, "I want to become a doctor next month and make $150k a year." They know many years of schooling is required to get a license. But yet these same people want to bypass the many years a successful entrepreneur has to put in (which is sometimes longer than a doctor) and go straight to $150k a year, starting at the end of the month. I guess it's ok to *want* that. We all do. I want a bag of money to fall into my yard. I've heard about this happening on two occasions, the story was on the show "Unsolved Mysteries." Unfortunately, this just isn't going to happen to us.

Whatever you want to achieve, don't just take my word for it, research for yourself stories about the most successful people in that business, or those who have achieved your goal. *How* did they get where they are? *Exactly* what did they do, and how long did it take? Whatever your research reveals, you have to be willing to do the *same thing*. If you're going to put in only 10% of the effort they put in, how could you possibly expect to achieve anything? You won't.

All hard work brings a profit, but mere talk leads only to poverty. (Proverbs 14:23)

I've heard a lot of stories about the MyPillow guying making hundreds of millions of dollars, and he did. But before his biz exploded, he sold his pillows at flea markets for several years, making next to nothing. Not to mention 20 years of prior failed businesses. Are you willing to do this with your business? Are you going to keep working and failing until you finally succeed? Or quit after a month, with a bunch of excuses.

A little sleep, a little slumber, a little folding of the hands to rest and poverty will come on you like a thief
and scarcity like an armed man. (Proverbs 6:10-11)

The choice to succeed is yours.

3. Develop Your Skills

Whatever business you start, you have to have some skills or experience in that business. This is common sense too, but how many people buy a bar or a restaurant and they've never had an employee, they can't cook or make a drink, they've never worked with customers, they've never marketed any business, they've never done ANYTHING!! And they expect to turn the business around. How is this possible?

Desire without knowledge is not good. How much more will hasty feet miss the way! (Proverbs 19:2)

You have to research and learn how your business works inside and out, *before* you buy/start it.

Would you take over the controls of an airplane mid-flight, and you've never been in an airplane cockpit before? You would if you wanted to die. But people do this exact same thing EVERY DAY with a business, and get the exact same result. An eventual crash landing!

I suggest *you* learn *at least* three main business skills that pertain to the business you're going to start. When I first started out as an online entrepreneur, I learned these three main business skills.

1. Marketing - You have to have some idea of what you're doing, so you can build a marketing game plan.
2. Website Creation - Not actually coding a site, just setting up a free Wordpress site.
3. Graphic Design - Just the basics to start. Editing photos, making basic logos and text graphics.

I learned three skills to start, and then continue to learn more.

The best doctors in the world right now, did they stop learning after they graduated from school 20-40 years ago? Of course not! If they did, they would know less about the new diseases than we do. Being the *best* requires a lifetime of learning.

Let the wise listen and add to their learning, and let the discerning get guidance. (Proverbs 1:5)

LearnBizOnline.com has many outstanding videos that will greatly help you, and cut down your learning time.

4. My Biz Philosophy

This is what "I" look for when I pick a business to get into, and I've done very well.

Of course you could go a different route, and max out your credit cards, mortgage your house, borrow $300,000 from your parents, family, and friends, and buy the local bar that you always wanted to own. It's a big investment, high risk, and you're limited to driving distance customers only. But you can do whatever you want. I myself, I'm looking for the *OPPOSITE!*

This is what I look for when starting a business:

> **Low Risk** - $1,000 or less to start the business.
> **High Reward** - Unlimited income potential.
> **Available To The World** - An online business.
> **Ground Floor Opportunity (low competition)** - This isn't a must, but for the most part, the pioneers (inventors) make the big bucks. The top people on the pyramid of Amway made millions. If you started Amway six months ago, good luck…

If you don't believe my $1,000 or less philosophy can make money, check out the free article on my website "How I Made Millions With $500" at OppJunk.com.

Here's a quick story. I saw a strip mall in California with two existing Mexican restaurants. One was a fast food Del Taco, and the other was a little more upscale, $20 a plate. The Del Taco did average business, and the more upscale Mexican restaurant did poorly. Well, another new Mexican restaurant opens up right between the two. Not upscale, just a step above Del Taco. Now there's three Mexican restaurants in a row. I'm not even going to tell you how the new restaurant did. It's common sense what's going to happen. Maybe I will tell you. I've never seen more than two people in there at one time, it's usually empty. The place was remodeled so nicely, it's an easy $150k loss when they close up in 6 months.

This is the *total opposite* of a ground floor opportunity. It's also extremely stupid. But it happens every day. Why? I have no idea.

5. Diversify Everything

You *don't* want to have only ONE business, using ONE advertising medium, and this is 100% your *only* source of income.

Even the big three automotive companies went bankrupt and lost everything, if it weren't for BILLION AND BILLIONS of dollars in government money given to them. Note - Ford took out BILLIONS in loans before the crash. This is PROOF that ANY business can FAIL! PERIOD.

I did this many years ago, and learned the hard way that every successful idea or business doesn't last forever.

Be sure you know the condition of your flocks, give careful attention to your herds; for riches do not endure forever and a crown is not secure for all generations. (Proverbs 27:23-24)

The problem is if the fad ends, or too many people copy your business, or when there's yet another recession, you could likely lose everything. You could have a successful brick and mortar business and two competitors might open exactly the same business within walking distance. That could be the beginning of the end for you.

The same goes for advertising/marketing. You could be #1 in Google search and they remove your listings, your streaming app loses huge traffic or closes up entirely (like periscope), or your social media account with 200,000 subscribers bans your account in the middle of the night. It happened to Trump, and he had over 80 million subscribers…

If you have only ONE place you advertise/promote your biz and this happens, you could lose ALL of your income in ONE DAY!

These two problems have happened to SO MANY businesses. Worldwide, it has happened to millions of business owners over the past 15 years.

Look at the "Painting & Wine" biz that made hundreds of millions of dollars around the country for a couple years, starting around 2015. I know a guy who had three locations and was making $200k a year. Basically, he spent the profits and once the fad ended he went belly up, losing everything.

But, what if he took that $400k profit and put $250K into online retail, or maybe tried a few low investment ideas from this book, and then put a little in the stock market? If he invested anything in 2015 his stock money quadrupled by now.

Do you get what I'm saying here? Give yourself a chance to be able to weather a storm with multiple revenue streams and solid diverse marketing plans. Even the Bible talked about this thousands of years ago.

Sow your seed in the morning, and at evening let your hands not be idle, for you do not know which will succeed, whether this or that, or whether both will do equally well. (Ecclesiastes 11:6)

Never Stop Starting

I had a dozen different titles for this article. Regardless of what I call it, my point is still the same.

Never stop saying, "I'm starting today, right now!"

I've heard so many motivational speakers talk about your "why," which is the driving force behind fulfilling your dreams. If it's too weak, you won't do what it takes.

The Bible talks about, *"Finishing being better than starting (Ecclesiastes 7:8)."* Very true.

This article is about STARTING! If you *never* start *anything,* your "why" is irrelevant, and "finishing" is *impossible.*

Starting begins with YOU saying, "TODAY IS THE DAY," and then you have to go for it.

But, you never know when THAT DAY really is. If you don't keep *starting,* THAT DAY will *never* come.

Here are few personal examples, so you get what I'm talking about.

I was 80lbs overweight weight from the age of 35-45. I've had a garage full of gym equipment (I periodically used) for my entire adult life. A couple times two a**hole neighbors laughed in my face, "Why do you have all this gym equipment? Hahahaha!" One of these guys was fatter than I was! And *he's* laughing at *me?*

Back to the story, 4-5 times a year for 10 years, I told a few people "today is the day! I'm starting my diet, working out, and I'm finally going to lose at least 50 lbs." Over and over, I started, did it for a few weeks and then quit.

But guess what? Eventually, there was a *last time* I said I was going to lose 50lbs. THAT WAS THE DAY! After 10 years, that was the day the weight loss journey finally began. I didn't give up this time. I lost the 50lbs in 9 months, and still kept it off to this day.

In my 20s, I said I was going to quit smoking 100 times. I even quit for a week, 20 times. Well, I haven't smoked in 25 years. One of the 100 times I said I was going to do it, the journey started that day.

I've created many successful businesses, video courses, books, Bible study programs, diet programs, and workouts. I don't think any of them went from start to finish. This is common, so don't get discouraged when this happens to you. Some were an idea in my head for several years, while others were start, quit, and then restart. But one day something finally clicked for each project, and I was able to complete them all. **"I never stopped starting."**

Disclaimer - Now, if anyone says 100+ times they are going to do something, that *does not* mean they *ever will*. It could just be talk for an entire lifetime.

You have to make a HUGE effort to break through the desire to quit, be willing to make sacrifices, and do whatever it takes.

But, if you quit after one failure or stop saying, "TODAY IS THE DAY," then *nothing* ever happens. Failure IS 100% guaranteed.

"No one can guarantee *success*, but we can all guarantee *failure*. Just say nothing, and do nothing." Pat Kennedy

Note - I actually saw that a**hole neighbor who laughed at me and my home gym, 15 years later. He could barely walk. We just looked at each other, neither saying a word. I didn't need to. And he definitely wasn't going to congratulate me. People like that never do. But that's fine. You don't need anyone's compliments or approval to succeed.

Regardless of what anyone says to you (or refuses to say), it has no bearing on your life. It's all irrelevant babble. They can't stop your destiny.

You have to either ignore the naysayers or use their words as fuel to achieve your goals. I was someone who did the latter.

Get back on your dream! Get that idea started! Start it up THIS WEEK and keep starting until you achieve your goal!

"You never know when THAT DAY really is. Just keep starting."

25 Best Biz Opportunities for 2022

25. Work From Home Jobs

Since this is technically not starting your own business, this is more of an FYI for someone who *quickly* needs an income, doesn't want to be exposed to Covid at a job, and doesn't have the time to build a business.

I'm just letting you know that many major companies like Amazon, Apple (Conduent.com), and Google are all hiring for work from home jobs at the time of the writing of this book. Customer service for many banks are now mostly work from home. I also know a couple people working from home for utility companies. Many companies discovered having their employees working from home saves them a lot of money, and it's now the wave of the future.

BIZ MARKET:
Great - Once again, work from home jobs are available now more than ever, and the future looks bright too.

LIKELY EARNING POTENTIAL:
Average - Apple customer service in 2022 pays $14/hr. Some companies pay a couple bucks more or less.

The pay could be considered poor for some jobs, but I raise the rating up to "average" because it's a blessing if you need to work from home because of Covid circumstances.

INITIAL INVESTMENT:
Low - Maybe $50 for a good customer service headset.

PROS:
- If you must work from home, this fulfills the need.
- Steady set income. Some people prefer guaranteed lower income, versus unstable income with huge upside.
- Once you open your eyes in the morning, you're at work! You could even work naked if you wanted too. Just don't pull a Jeffrey Toobin if people can see you!
- And never forget (with any job), you can always build a more profitable business or work on a passive income project after you get off work.

CONS:
- Pay is decent, but usually isn't great.
- It's a 40 hour a week job, working for the man (though you may never see him in person).
- Some of these "work from home" companies will fire you for *anything*. They have 1000's of employees and a lot of times the management is *extremely poor.*

FINAL THOUGHTS:

Like I said, it's a job but it might be a great blessing for some. Pick an industry you like and research if they're hiring. Also research company reviews from previous employees. If half the former employees say the company totally sucks, it probably does…

Obviously, start with highest paying companies factoring in job requirements/former employee reviews.

24. Mobile PC/Laptop Repair & Used Sales

I just lumped this all together. Right now there's HUGE potential with multiple computers needed in many homes, and lower income families looking for cheaper options. And down the road, more computers in the market place means more potential clients for repairs and upgrades.

I'm pretty good with computers *now*, but 15 years ago if my hard drive failed or a virus destroyed the system, I called a mobile PC repair company.
They would charge me $200 for a hard drive and a fresh copy of windows, and $75 labor to install them. The entire job took 1-1.5 hrs, mainly waiting for windows to install. I was told by the repair guys that this type of work was the bulk of their business.

This is yet another one of those businesses where if you ever thought about getting into it, now is the time!

BIZ MARKET:
Good - Computer repair and used PC sales will always be needed.

LIKELY EARNING POTENTIAL:
Good - $75 to $100 per home. Plus parts markup, installing hardware extras, and used computer sales. A few hundred a day profit is definitely possible.

INITIAL INVESTMENT:
Medium - Maybe several hundred bucks for on-hand stock. You can run out and pick everything up as needed when you're first starting out, which reduces your initial start-up costs.

PROS:
- Another biz where if you love this kind of stuff, it's a blessing to be able to do it for a living. It's not even work if you love doing it.
- You could learn pretty much all you need to know about this biz in a month. LearnBizOnline.com has many great computer repair courses.
- Most jobs will be quick easy money.

CONS:
- Possible irate customers when you tell them their data can't be saved.
- Though most of your jobs will be easy hardware swapouts, upgrades, and reinstalls, you *will* occasionally get one of those "I don't know WTF is wrong" jobs. Not fun.

But then again, you will be asking callers/emailers what's wrong with their PC before you visit them. You could always decline the tough jobs, and only take the easy ones.

FINAL THOUGHTS:

I always wanted to start this business, even as a side job. But I just don't like going inside a stranger's house and working. I know millions of people do this for a living in many fields of work, but it's just not for me. If *you* don't mind it, this business has great potential in 2022 and beyond.

23. Elderly Home Care Service

This job entails shopping, errand running, picking up prescriptions, and basic help like washing clothes, a little house cleaning, maybe cooking, taking out the trash, getting meds together, and maybe some companionship time.

I know someone who works at a commercial Home Instead caregiver company. Some locations do well, and some don't. Regardless, there's a gap in home care service industry that needs to be filled.

Most commercial caregiver companies require at least four consecutive hours a day, and two days a week minimum at $25-$30/hr. This is good for some, but many clients want two hours a day for 5-7 days a week. This is where the gap that you can fill comes.

You could go $20/hr with a 2hr minimum. With only a 2hr minimum, driving time cuts into the profits. But, if you can schedule clients no more than 30 minutes apart, the money works. This $20 price point still leaves some meat on the bone if you decide to hire employees at $10/hr.

Note - Be sure to check licensing in your city before starting this business.

BIZ MARKET:
Good - There will always be elderly and persons with disabilities who need assistance. The early 2022 Covid months will increase the need for the errand running part of the business.

LIKELY EARNING POTENTIAL:
Average - If you can book several accounts and hire a few employees, you can move this up to "great." Otherwise, it's just average if you're on your own.

INITIAL INVESTMENT:
Low - If you have transportation, you're good to go.

PROS:
- You can set your own hours (for the most part).
- This type of work is fulfilling for many. You're not getting paid big bucks, but you're making a positive impact on someone's life while getting paid for it, with no boss hanging over you.

CONS:
- Some clients will be challenging to work with and demanding. But, I guess that's with any business.
- You will have clients who will call you all hours of the day. Some will expect you to drop everything for their needs.

FINAL THOUGHTS:

We all need money to survive, but money isn't *everything*. You can't take it with you when you die. But what you did good for others here on this earth, *that lives on forever*.

22. Home Child Day Care Service

To some extent, I've done at least 75% of the businesses in this book. But this one, NEVER!

But, I do know a couple people who did this with 3-4 children they cared for every week. This is how I knew it was feasible that it could even be done.

Note - Please check you local licensing laws before getting too deep into this business. It may be too complicated, or not even possible in your city or state.

Like I mentioned before, this one is purely an idea. I can't help too much with this one. You will have to put in some research. There are a few sites online that get into this biz pretty good.

BIZ MARKET:
Great - *Affordable* child day care is *always* a great need. People want affordable "anything." That's why the Walmart heirs each have $15+ billion in their pockets. Cheap wins!

LIKELY EARNING POTENTIAL:
Great - Rates vary from state to state, but for a Med-Lrg sized state the going rate is $350-$450 a week per child. Four children brings in roughly $80k a year.

INITIAL INVESTMENT:
Medium - You'll need door gates, a play pen, throw rugs, maybe a crib or a high chair, toys, an extra TV, just to name a few things. $500-$1,000. You can always add items as money comes in.

PROS:
- $80k a year income that doesn't require 4-10 years of college. Not bad.
- I know a few people who really love children. This could be a blessing, and like free money for them.

CONS:
- Licensing could be a problem in a few cities.
- Some children could have serious health or behavioral issues.
- What if a child gets injured or sick while under your supervision.

FINAL THOUGHTS:
This might be a great business for you if your city allows it. Earn money, and make a positive influence on a child's life. That's a win win!

21. Dog Sitter or Walker

I'm listing this job because it's a great easy part-time opportunity that works very well for many.

Rover.com is the Uber/Air BnB for dog sitting and walking. Check out their many positive reviews on Indeed.

Get together your pics (with your pets) for your Rover.com profile, and then decide your hours and what you would like to offer.

BIZ MARKET:
Poor to Great - Depends on the city you live in.

LIKELY EARNING POTENTIAL:
Average - From what I can gather online, looks like a few hundred dollars a week. I rate it as "average" because its a part-time gig and very easy work.

Also, you could work on another passive income stream like ebooks, e-courses, blogging, YouTube videos, etc. while making money with dogs sleeping in your kitchen.

INITIAL INVESTMENT:
Low - Signing up at Rover.com is free. Maybe extra cleaning supplies.

PROS:
- Easy work, if you want to even call it work.
- Work will be booming in some cities.
- You choose the days and time frame.
- You can multi-task with other businesses while baby sitting dogs.

CONS:
- Multiple dogs in your house might fight.
- Work could be scarce in some cities.
- Transfer of fleas within your house is likely (flea meds are an easy fix).
- You might not realize a dog is peeing in your house until it's too late!
- God forbid a dog gets off its leash and gets injured or lost.
- You could also get shot, if you're walking French bulldogs. It is possible.

FINAL THOUGHTS:
This is a great opportunity that will work well for many pet lovers.

20. Rent Out Your Property

This is a great passive income opportunity for some, if possible. Because of rents skyrocketing, many people will be evicted in 2022, or just low on funds. There will be a need for cheaper rental and storage options. Renting out a spare room or part of your garage for storage could be very beneficial for both parties.

BIZ MARKET:
Great - 2022 might be the best year ever, If you've ever thought about giving this a try. I know a couple people who just bought houses for Airbnb rental properties only.

LIKELY EARNING POTENTIAL:
Great - I say "great" because it's passive income. Renting out a room in your home, you can get $600-$1,000 a month. Maybe more if the room is a huge master bedroom in a great area.

Airbnb room rental goes for $50-$75+ a day, but could be much more depending on your city and demand.

You could rent out a portion of your garage for a couple hundred bucks a month for storage. If you're not using it, it's free money.

INITIAL INVESTMENT:
Low - Unless you have to furnish the entire room, it's free to use what you already have. Well, maybe a camera system ($300-$500). Actually, this is a must. Many Airbnb hosts have a camera system for liability and anti-theft purposes. It's also a deterrent, and proof if ever needed.

PROS:
- Passive income is nice!
- You don't need to learn any skills, or have to go to school for this one.
- You can advertise for free on Craigslist, Rentme or on the Airbnb app.

CONS:
- A renter could bring Covid into your house.
- A drunk Airbnb guest could piss the bed and soak the mattress all the way through. Tip - Get a plastic mattress cover.
- There's always the chance of theft when you're not home, or they could set your house on fire by mistake. Or on purpose.
- Or even worse, they could wait for you to come out of your bedroom in the morning and kill you.

I think I've been watching too many Unsolved Mysteries lately. But then again, I'm just keeping it real…

FINAL THOUGHTS:

This was all sounding like a great biz opportunity until I got to the cons. But for most people, this will work out very well.

19. E-Restaurant / Gourmet Food Delivery

In 2021, I saw several stories about companies (a few were startups) in Los Angeles who were cooking food in their kitchen or garage, and they were doing very well.

One guy (who was fairly established in the area before Covid) claimed he was selling 5,000 dinners a week! This is hard for me to believe, but even if he embellished his sales by 60%, and was really selling only 2,000 dinners a week, that's $1.3 million profit a year! Note - The news story did show him packing about 75 to go containers on every counter in his kitchen. *He's making money.*

Another company made organic healthy foods. Organic salads filled with fresh fruits and vegetables. Top of the line ingredients used to create delicious healthy dishes. This company was also doing very well.

A few observations of these successful businesses. They made good *quality* food you couldn't make at home in five minutes. They weren't delivering hot dogs, $2 street tacos, or canned spaghetti.

The $1.3 million dollar man wasn't serving frozen raviolis (though I love frozen raviolis). He rolled out the dough, cut it into squares, put a filling between them and crimped it closed to create a fresh ravioli. And the sauce wasn't Ragu either. *Real tomatoes* were used in the creation of his sauce.

From the stories I saw on the LA news the last several months, a lot of people in *this city* are willing to pay $25-$40 for top notch high quality meals, and are trying out a lot of new places.

BIZ MARKET:
Good - Carry outs, uber eats, and eating restaurant food at home have all become very popular in 2021, and will still be in 2022. I'm not saying people now prefer it to dining out, I'm just saying so many new customers have been exposed to it, it's no longer new to them. This makes the food delivery market bigger than ever.

LIKELY EARNING POTENTIAL:

Good - The food business is a tough business. I rate earning potential as "good" because I saw several companies making $100k plus a year doing this. But I'm sure many will try this and bust out. Then again, that's with any business. There are many factors for success here.

INITIAL INVESTMENT:

Medium (to start) - Once this gets going a bit you'll need an extra freezer, a fridge or two, mixers, extra pots and pans, etc. That's a few thousand dollars.

Now of course, as you make money you can use it to expand as needed. The entire amount isn't due day one. It's actually a *good thing* when you need to buy the third freezer and have the money for it!

PROS:
- Unlimited income potential.
- You could be fulfilling a lifelong dream.
- A great feeling of accomplishment if you succeed with this tough start up.
- Was there ever a better time to start this business?

CONS:
- Most restaurant businesses fail. Even if the food is amazing. It's a tough business.
- Licensing could cost a bit. Be sure to check out the requirements before you start.
- Requires long hours and hard work, if you want even a shot at doing well.
- Cooking requires talent, and great judgment of what tastes good and what doesn't.
- You could serve someone rotten food and they could have diarrhea for three days.

Note - If you don't pay attention to food temps and expiration dates, *please* include a free roll of toilet paper with every meal.

FINAL THOUGHTS:

If you've ever wanted to sell meals to the public, now might be the best time in your life to give it a shot.

Selling food made at home is way cheaper than owning a restaurant. You're looking at a few grand versus a few hundred grand (if you count having some reserve rent on hand).

If you start this business and do well, email me and let me know - **Pat@OppJunk.com**

18. Moving Company

Many people are downsizing their homes or moving to a cheaper city. California is seeing over 100k people a year moving to Las Vegas, Texas, Florida and Tennessee. Some will permanently lose their jobs and be forced to move to another city or state that best suits their job skills. Moving companies are *badly needed* in 2022.

In mid 2020, I saw a story about a California long distance moving company. The owner said they were booked a solid six weeks in advance. He's been in business 20 years, and said he's never seen this many people moving before. Not even close.

Before dismissing this as an impossible business opportunity, it's easier than you think. A few of the moving companies I hired in Las Vegas, they just rented a Uhaul truck and grabbed some day workers from Home Depot to do the moving. It always worked out very well and everyone got paid.

One moving company I hired had the real John Wayne Bobbit working for them as a mover. You remember this guy, right? He's the guy whose wife cut off his penis, drove down the street with it in her hand, and then threw it in a field. A police dog ended up finding it, and a doctor sewed back on what he could.

I told him, he's lucky *my dog* didn't find his wiener in the field, he would have thought it was a Vienna sausage and eaten it! 110% guaranteed! No way it would've made it to the doctor's office in one piece.
Needless to say, Mr. Bobbit was not amused by my comments. He said it wasn't funny, he almost died from blood loss. But he was still nice enough to sign an autograph for my mom. He drew a knife under his signature with blood dripping. Really!

BIZ MARKET:
Great to Poor - This rating is "city based." *Some cities* like California, Nevada, Florida and others will have a *great* need for movers. While others in the south and various areas will have *zero* need.

LIKELY EARNING POTENTIAL:
Great to Poor - Once again this is city based. I know the moving companies I worked with in Las Vegas did very very well. Rough profit estimate - the owner ran two trucks 5 days a week, 10 hours a day. They charged $75/hour x 50 hours is $3,750 a week. Truck rental, gas, and $10/hr for employees is about $1,250 a week. That's $130k a year profit running two trucks. But what if you ran four trucks?

INITIAL INVESTMENT:

Low - Truck rental $40-$60 a day. Gas and employee wages (you get this from the client after the job is finished).

Note - I don't know if this owner had a license or if he was even insured. He did have a contract and official looking company paperwork. And they did a great job. But even if he had to pay these fees and it costs him an extra $500 a month, he's still banking over $100k a year.

PROS:
- A contractor type job that doesn't require much experience.
- Great earning potential is possible, especially if you rent multiple trucks in a booming city.
- Anyone can move furniture.

CONS:
- Bottom of the barrel workers means there's a better chance they might not show up or come in drunk/high. Or God forbid they steal the whole moving truck filled with a client's belongings and never come back! Note - John Wayne Bobbit and his cousin both smelled like hard liqour. He said whiskey was his energy drink. Ha!
- So many people will be moving in some cities, available rental trucks might be hard to find. If you get into this business, you *must* work out a monthly rental deal or sign a contact guaranteeing your trucks will be there every morning. *I would make sure this is possible first before anything else.*
- Some cities just won't have any business.

FINAL THOUGHTS:

This is a great biz opportunity for the right person in the right city. And if you open this in Las Vegas, maybe John Wayne Bobbit will apply.

17. Online Recording Studio

My buddy John Rogers, from JRmastering.com, has been doing mixing, mastering, and podcast editing since 1999, and has done very well. He's worked with over 9,000 customers all over the world, and it's all done via Wetransfer.com fileshare.

Of course you'll have to learn some skills for this business. RecordingStudioSecrets.com is the best book to learn how to make money with an online recording studio. Also, LearnBizOnline.com is another amazing resource that will help you learn the craft.

BIZ MARKET:
Good - There's a lot of competition in this business, but so many new people are working with online recording studios right now because the local walk in studios are closed. They have no other choice.

Many artists have purchased their own music equipment. They're finding they can record at home, and then have everything mixed and mastered online, bypassing the local recording studio all together. Plus they save 50% too. This trend will continue to grow for years to come.

Also, more people are making podcasts, which means more episodes need to be edited.

LIKELY EARNING POTENTIAL:
Good - $25k/year is easily attainable (within a year) if you work hard to build your clientele, and do a good job (so they come back). That's not a ton of money, but I rank it as "good" because it only requires a 15-20 hour work week to earn $25k/year. This leaves a lot of time to create other passive income opportunities.

INITIAL INVESTMENT:
Medium - You'll need a computer, a decent speaker setup, an audio interface, DAW software, and plugin software. A brand new decent setup, you're looking at $4,000. If you get some refurbished items and use several free software products, make it $800.

Note - I *highly* recommend a refurbished computer from Amazon (if you need a PC for *any* biz). I bought a few very nice ones from Amazon at 75% off. They were all near mint condition inside and out. A shockingly great purchase! They also come with a 3 month warranty, but I've never had to use it. Be sure to check the reviews for whichever company you choose to buy from.

PROS:
- Decent money for a part-time job, and you set your own hours.
- If you're into music, you're getting paid to do what you love. FREE MONEY!
- You'll meet great people in the music business.
- It's a repeat customer business. Good clients will come back every few months for years.
- There are many great resources online to help you learn the business.

CONS:
- If you suck at it, you will get a lot of refund requests and no repeat customers.
- There's a learning curve to get good at this. Your customers will let you know where your skills rate.
- Like any service business, it will take time to build your clientele base.

FINAL THOUGHTS:

Do what you love and meet great people too. Even if it's only a part-time gig, becoming an online recording studio engineer is a great career choice in 2022.

16. Sports Handicapping Service

This business is predicting winning sports teams versus the Las Vegas points spread. Gamblers bet on your predictions and hopefully make money (if you're good).

As a sports handicapper, you don't pick "*every game*" that would dilute any advantage you have. You only release a few selections to your customers. Selections you feel have the best chance of winning.

I ran this business for a few years in the late 90's and did extremely well. But I was an outstanding sports handicapper That immensely helps.

BIZ MARKET:
Good - This pie is cut up into at least a few hundred slices, but several states have just legalized sports gambling which increase the pie size. You're getting 1,000's of fresh new bettors who have never gambled on sports before.

LIKELY EARNING POTENTIAL:
Great - If you're good at this, income potential is *incredible*. Many sports bettors wager a lot of money. If your picks are solid, these guys will win a few thousand a month. They'll give you $500 a month, no questions asked, if you can make them money. Only fifty regular clients and you're making *big bank!*

Obviously the key is winning. If you suck, a client will pay you only once.

INITIAL INVESTMENT:
Low - Nothing more than the basics.

PROS:
- Easy big money for some.
- Clients are beyond happy with you when you win, and they will let you know it.
- Not hard to get new clients if you give out free picks and they win.

CONS:
- This business is one of the most scammmer ridden businesses ever created. One step below Ponzi schemer. I'm just saying the business has a terrible reputation.
- You have to know what you're doing. If your picks are worse than what they can pick on their own, they don't need you to help them lose more money!

- One bad week (or one game they loaded up on) and some clients act like it's the end of the world. And they will let you know it!
- It's tough to learn how to pick winners. Watch the NFL announcer predictions. Most can't even win 50% of their games, with no spread.
- No matter what picks you give your clients, many will always find a way to lose, and then blame you.

Quick true story. When I did this in the 90s, my football picks were RED HOT for several weeks. This guy sends me $100 for my college and pro picks for the weekend. I told him, I *really* like these games this weekend. And I did.

Sat I went 4-0, Sun 5-1, Mon 0-1. That's 9-2 (82%) for my clients over the weekend. That's as good as you will *ever* get from a sports handicapper.

The guy calls me on Tuesday, "F this, F that, you make me sick you MF!" I replied, "WHAT?!?! I went 9-2!" You didn't get my picks?"

This is a true story.

He tells me he didn't believe I would win. *But yet he gave me $100.* Stupid.

He then tells me he bet his own picks. On Saturday, he went 1-5, and lost $2,200. Sunday his picks lost $4,000. Monday he noticed I went 8-1 over the weekend. Down $6,200 with his own picks, he bets $10k on my Monday night pick. It losses..

Recap - The guys buys my picks for $100, they go 9-2 and he LOSSES $16,200.

Unfortunately, this happens very often. Or what they do is they bet only the games they agree with. I go 8-3 and of course they agreed with only three games, the three losers. Which makes sense. These guys pick losers so well, that whatever they agree with they should bet the opposite!

Note - One weekend I went 8-0 in the NFL. *NO ONE* lost that week! I hope...

FINAL THOUGHTS:

This is an idea book, but I will give you two sports handicapping tips that helped me immensely last season.

First off, any team can cover the spread any week. Get this in your head and don't forget it. In 2020, yes the Raiders DID beat KC. Should have done it twice. Things like this *can* happen.

Second, after you spend a long time studying and evaluating a game, if you're completely undecided, take the points. I won SO many games doing this in 2020. Many times a team was giving 3-5 points on the road, and I wasn't even sure they would win the game outright. And most of the time they didn't. I took the points and did *very* well.

I won the 2020 Superbowl with this tip. KC and Tampa already played in 2020 and KC won by only three. Close game. It was unlikely Tyreke Hill will amass 269 yards and 3 tds like he did in the first meeting. After that debacle, obviously he would be triple teamed, which will greatly reduce those numbers. And Tampa's defense is very good.

On the flip side, Mahomes wins so many games like this. And Tampa wasn't expected to score a lot of points.

"Either team could win this," though I was leaning *slightly* towards Tampa. Tampa +3.5 at home. Take the points. It was a very easy win.

15. Content Provider

With more business websites coming online, there's a huge need for fresh original content if the owner doesn't have time, doesn't want to, or can't write it.

For those of you who aren't familiar with SEO (Search Engine Optimization), fresh original content is a factor that accounts for a website's search engine ranking on Google. You can't rank high in the search engines with a one page business website. You need consistent original content being produced. This content also brings in traffic through web pages other than the homepage.

Some business owners don't even know they need this for SEO. Many create a one page website and few product pages, make it live on the Internet, and call it a day. It doesn't work that way if you want high search engine rankings and free traffic.

And of course the obvious reason, constant fresh content *brings back return visitors* wanting to see what's new.

Sites like MakeALivingWriting.com, Scripted.com, Upwork.com, Fiver.com, Freelancer.com allow you to either bid, apply, or see available writing jobs. Many various freelance gigs are here. Check these sites out!

BIZ MARKET:
Average - Demand is high, but available dirt cheap content providers are everywhere! You have people in third world countries working for a few dollars an hour rewriting other people's articles. That's your competition.

This is a classic "get what you pay for" scenario. If you pay nothing, you get back garbage. Many times the grammar is extremely poor. But some business owners don't see the value in paying more for a good writer who produces great original content that people will actually like and come back for.

LIKELY EARNING POTENTIAL:
Good - There's a lot of potential here if you can hook up with a few decent paying companies needing long term content, like 2-3 articles a week each. But if you can only find part-time work, being a content writer is still good use of your time.

If you can write well, split your time between the *service* part of the business and *creating* your own ebooks and information/social blogs. Why, because these are passive income sources and eventually you could make $1,000 a week without having to do anything other than promoting your own products.

If you do this you're also diversifying your income. God forbid you get sick, you'll still have money coming in. If all your businesses are *service only* businesses, if you can't do the service, you don't get paid.

With any business, always build for long term growth and increase your business diversity as much as you can.

INITIAL INVESTMENT:
Low - $400 for a cheap laptop. For pure writing, the best cheap laptop I've ever owned in my life is the Asus ImagineBook. It surfs the net very well too. For under $400, it's an outstanding laptop.

PROS:
- Do what you love!
- This is one of those "take your laptop to the coffee shop or park" type of jobs. A true blessing!
- It's good practice for your own projects and websites.
- Writing commercially gives you at least a small feeling of accomplishment.

CONS:
- It takes time to get established, but it will be well worth it in the long run if you put the time in.
- In some markets, you'll have to compete with a third world country wage scale.
- *Talent* is required, though a lot can be learned.

FINAL THOUGHTS:

If you want to start a career in content writing, hustle and get after it! Apply for many content writing jobs, start your own blog, and write your first ebook. Do it all in 2022! Why not?

And once you do, please email me your success story! **Pat@OppJunk.com**

14. Online Marketing Specialist

Whether directly or indirectly, the goal of this job is to help the company earn more money with their products or services. Even if you're just managing social media accounts, the ultimate goal is to get more subscribers/traffic, which should eventually translate into profits for the company. If someone is paying you, none of this is done for fun or leisure. Results are rightfully expected.

Let me briefly explain several facets of online marketing. You could specialize in one or all of them. The more the merrier. Note - This biz idea book explains "what" they are. I could write an entire book on "how" to do each one.

SEO (Search Engine Optimization) -
The goal here is to improve the Google search engine ranking of website pages for specific keywords. If you did the best job possible, when someone types a specific keyword (that you determine) into Google search, the client's website page comes up as the #1 listing. This isn't a requirement, Top 10 is a more realistic goal, but #1 is the ultimate goal.

FYI - SEO isn't *only* for the homepage. A*ll* of the pages in a website should rank high for a specific keyword set that you designate.

Social Media Manager
Basically, you're running all the social media sites for a company. You're creating fresh content, updating when needed, replying to comments and emails, you're the social media voice of the company. Your goal is to increase subscribers and bring repeat visitors by providing creative and high quality content. This job usually includes running the paid social media ad campaigns too.

Note - I mentioned a few different social media services here. You can offer a few or all of them. It's up to you. You don't have to offer everything, but it's to your advantage if you do. Companies like to keep things all under *one* roof. Why hire three different social media companies when *one* could do it all?

Social Media Subscriber (Subs) & Traffic Builder
This specific marketing facet is different than the social media manager. You are paid to bring in legit subscribers and/or traffic to social media accounts, by whatever means you have. Most of the time you never have admin access to any of the social sites. You're just sending them traffic and acquiring subs.

Some companies will want "real" people who interact and revisit their websites. Others will settle for fake traffic, they just want *numbers,* so ask the customer what their specific needs are.

But, *ALL* companies want the work you perform to *stick* and not get their account banned for life! You have to learn the ins and outs on how this works before hand. Not by trial and error on paying clients' accounts.

Purchasing Effective Ads & Running Effective Ad Campaigns
This is self explanatory. Your clients are expecting to turn a profit from the ads you purchase for them.

Start short ad campaigns for your clients, and then quickly adjust to improve effectiveness based on results. Note - You *should be* getting decent results right off the bat because *you've done this before.*

A Few Marketing Companies I've Dealt With
I've dealt with a few scam marketing companies and they all started out with, "What's your budget?" I told them my budget, and they e-mail me a marketing plan that spends the entire amount. That's *normal* for marketing companies.

What wasn't normal was the fact that many of the sites wanted me to advertise on were obscure (probably owned by them), PPC ads were too much money per click that I couldn't mathematically turn a profit, and there was no mention about effectiveness or what return I could expect to get back.

It was basically just paying someone to randomly spend all of my ad money in one day on any site that sells ads, not having *any* knowledge on what results I could expect . ANYONE could do that themselves for free! Note - I never used any of these companies. The scam was too obvious.

To be good in this business, you have to have experience with other clients, know advertising mediums on and offline, have run various ad campaigns in different genres, etc. You have to know what works and what doesn't, to some extent. *That's why you're getting paid!*

BIZ MARKET:
Good - The need for good marketers is *BEYOND* great! But, there are sooo many scam companies doing this, some guaranteeing 50,000 visitors for $5 and yielding zero results. This gives the business a bad name.

Note - See my "Final Thoughts" at the end of this article for my marketing philosophy that will help you shed the bad name.

LIKELY EARNING POTENTIAL:
Great - If you're very good at marketing, you can make a TON of money. You can make even more if you market *your own* products.

INITIAL INVESTMENT:
Low - Just the basics.

PROS:
- The skies the limit when it comes to earning potential.
- If you learn marketing, you can create unlimited income streams for yourself and market them all!

CONS:
- There's a lot to learn here for a beginner. Trial and error is involved early on, and *someone* will lose money.
- It's hard to convince a client you can achieve results without a free sample, though I don't consider this a bad thing. It allows you to charge more once they experience your *great* results.
- It takes time for *free* social marketing to work, no matter how great you are. Whether it's Google search results, Youtube, FB, IG, etc. it takes months, not weeks, to become a player in the market place.
- The entire Online Marketing industry has a bad name. Most companies in this biz are scammers that send out countless spam emails, they deliver fake traffic, or yield poor results with whatever they provide. Below I show you how to beat the bad rap.

FINAL THOUGHTS:

"Help someone legitimately make money. As long as you do, they will gladly keep giving you some of it." - Pat Kennedy

This is my marketing philosophy, and I 110% guarantee it works!

Most marketing companies (any businesses in general) use a different wordly philosophy.

"If you can effectively lie to a potential client and trick them into believing you, you can scam them out of their money." Their only goal is to find gullible people and exploit them.

How I Made Over $100k Using An "Honest" Marketing Strategy
In 1998, I had a legit sports handicapping website. If you don't know what this is, sports handicapping is predicting the outcome (who is going to win) of sporting events against the Las Vegas point spread. A good sports handicapping service wins a high percentage of their picks. These picks are sold to bettors.

One of my websites was a directory of sports handicappers. At the time, Yahoo and AOL were the search engine kings. It was VERY easy to get a #1 search engine ranking with them for any keyword you wanted. I was getting about 10,000 visitors a day for FREE, and dominated the much smaller than now Internet market.

My idea was to sell ad space in the directory to other sports handicappers. I put my visitor stats on the sales page and was charging $200 a month.

I was personally making over $10k a month from this website with my own service, so I knew for a fact $200 a month was an absolute STEAL price for new advertisers. I was such a good handicapper, I wasn't concerned with adding competition. I just wanted ten handicappers paying me a total of $2k a month passive income.

Well, after 2 months I got ZERO advertisers to sign-up. Nada.

I KNEW FOR A FACT my sports handicapper directory would be *HIGHLY EFFECTIVE* for *any* sports handicapper. I couldn't just sit there and do nothing. I had to try *something!*

So, I decided to give it away for free! "Give it away, give it away, give it away, now!" What did I have to lose? I was already making $0. It doesn't get any lower than that.

A business associate said to me, "No one gives advertising away for free. I've never seen this before in my life. Just lower the price to $100." Nooope! He can now say he saw it *once* in his life...

Back to the story. Right at the start of the football season the deal was a FREE home page banner for a full month. At the end of the month, it was $1,000 a month advertising fee. Five handicappers took me up on this offer.

From the sales I personally made through my website and just talking to the advertisers, I could tell they were all making $4-$6k profit a month. As expected (but still a little surprising) the ads were *highly* effective for everyone. I legitimately made them money. They were super excited to pay me the $1k at the start of each month because that meant they made another $3-$5k for basically a part-time side hustle.

Over the next 2 months I added more handicappers and eventually had a total of ten, and then capped it at that (so everyone made decent money each month).

I ended up making $10k a month passive income from these guys for about 2 years.

I also did the same thing with the top *online sports betting site*. Free advertising for a month. The manager there told me they made over $100k from the traffic my website brought in (and these are repeat customers). They ended paying me a flat salary of $15k a month for about 3 years.

$15k a month might sound like a lot you, but I made them millions! There was one guy who owned a huge Wisconsin cheese factory who loved to bet *big* on sports. He lost $100k a month like clock work. Rumor had it, he was making over a million a month profit with his cheese, so the high losses were nothing to him.

Back to my main point. I know from personal experience, **"If you make someone some money, they will gladly give you some if it!"**

Over a thousand companies the last 20 years have offered to help me sell my products or promote my online services, or asked me to advertise on their websites. I asked all of them, "Give me a week free. I used to give potential clients a free month. If your service/website ads are so great, I'll make money that week, and then I will start paying you." Makes sense to me. If you're that great, prove it.

Nope. NOT ONE COMPANY in 20 years would offer me a free week. ZERO. Most wanted at least 3 months, which was $1,000 minimum. Why? Because they knew my results would be $0. They wanted to squeeze as much cash out of me as they could because they knew I would *never* renew. A free week is a waste of time.

If your whole business is lies and bullshit, you're basically a scam. Whatever it takes, learn how to become great in your field of business. Why not do the work it takes and make a lot of money, honestly?

13. Financial Advisor

This section focuses on the upcoming "need" for financial advisors, not on tips for running this business.

In 2020-21 many Americans were bailed out by government funds, but MILLIONS were not. And some who were, wasted all the money with nothing to show for it.

Bottom line, millions of people will need good financial advice, and a game plan that will help them get their lives back together.

BIZ MARKET:
Great - I'm saying *great* because giving financial advice has always been a lucrative business, even during good economic times. Now *millions* of potential clients have been added to the client pool.

LIKELY EARNING POTENTIAL:
Great - Any successful advisor, counselor, life coach, etc. that "I" know all make good money for little work. $50-$100 an hour would be the bare minimum rate. Usually financial advisors print up an entire financial game plan for $500+. Some even have a course they sell along with the game plan. You could also include services (for an extra fee) like negotiating with the credit card companies or the IRS in efforts to reduce the balance.

INITIAL INVESTMENT:
Low - Website, computer with Internet, printer, phone and you're in business.

PROS:
- Many have made a *tremendous* amount of money from this business genre, even during *good* economic times.
- You can do it by yourself from home. No employees required.

CONS:
- To the general consumer, this business has scam written all over it. Most *are* scams, and it might be tough getting someone to trust you. I said "tough" but it *can* be done. Like I already mentioned, *many* do very well with this biz.

FINAL THOUGHTS:
When looking to start a new business, potential clients are one of the main factors you look for. And, if it's low investment risk too, that makes it even better. This business has it all!

12. Create Royalty Free Products

How this business works is, people need royalty free music, beats, photos, video clips, graphics or website templates mainly for their commercials, ads, book covers, YouTube videos or websites.

They don't want to "own" your work, for a fee they are granted a license to "use" your work on a limited basis. Example - Your song plays in the background of their commercial, or your photo appears within one of their blog articles, or someone sings/raps to your original instrumentals.

Ok, this business genre is pretty much played out. Each pie is cut up into literally over a million slices.

The only reason I'm including it is because you might already have a portfolio ready to go, and all income is passive. All you have to do is create your accounts and upload your material. You might do very well.

The other reason I included this biz is because it's such a popular passive source of income, I want you to know the truth about it, and not have any unrealistic expectations.

Maybe after reading this you will decide it's best for you to put your time, money, and efforts into something else.

Here are a few popular websites to get you started, but there are way more than these.

Lease Your Music, Commercial Jingles & Beats
Pond5.com, AudioJungle.com, Envato.com

Note - I have five songs on Pond5.com, I uploaded them like 6 years ago. They still send me $100 twice a year. I'm not getting rich, but I'm not doing *anything* for this money either.

But what if *you* uploaded 200 songs? That's $150 a week for doing nothing, and that's from only *one* website, Pond5.com. Upload all 200 songs to *several* royalty free music websites, now that's a decent amount of free passive income.

Lease Your Photos, Images, Video Clips, Graphics, Website Templates
Dreamstime.com, Envato.com, Shutterstock.com

BIZ MARKET:
Average - The market is super saturated but it continues to grow and will be around forever.

LIKELY EARNING POTENTIAL:
Low - The pie is cut up so much here you might not even be able to get a super thin slice. Maybe just a strawberry or a cherry, or some crumbs in a few genres. But it's passive income, which is good. Anything passive is worth taking a shot at if the price vs time is right.

Like I mentioned, your income vastly increases if you can upload hundreds of items that are already ready to go. If you can do this, bump my earnings rating to "Good."

INITIAL INVESTMENT:
Low - I'm going low because I'm suggesting this business for someone who's already in it, and has all the equipment they need.

If you need to buy music equipment, camera equipment, need to learn how to use it all, etc. I *wouldn't* suggest spending $2k to work solely in this business. You might never recoup it. This is a passive side gig.

Unless of course you can change the industry with something unique, and can upload a ton of material. If you can do this, go all out with it!

PROS:
- For a third time, it's passive income, with no boss.
- You're selling your passion. It's very satisfying when you can do this.
- Commissions roll in for a long time. I'm going on six years making money with my handful of songs.

CONS:
- Only crumbs are left in the pie pan for many genres/markets.
- If you go in the wrong direction (like create material for a proven weak genre), you could earn nothing.

FINAL THOUGHTS:
To make money in the royalty free market; You *don't* create what *YOU* love, and expect people to buy it. You *find out* what *THEY* love (want) and create something great based on this info.

Look at different genres/categories and do keyword searches on royalty free websites. Then sort by "best sellers." What are people buying? What should you stay away from? Base your creations on this data. Business related images are usually hot, nature photos not so much. Commercial type jingles are always hot for royalty free music. Base your creations on *best seller* data.

Video clips are really expensive, $50-$100+. Maybe target that market and come in at $30-$40, undercutting the entire market. It's a thought. "Do the proper research for any business you plan on getting into."

11. Release Your Music CD

This is another business suggestion that isn't exactly a *"great"* business idea from a financial standpoint. It's more of an *achievement* based idea I felt should be included in this book.

It's a great lifetime achievement for someone who has talent, and has always wanted to do this. Also, a great way to express the gifts God gave them.

I've heard so many people say they want to make their own CD "one day" or at least make a song. Let 2022 be the year you *finally* get it done!

BIZ MARKET:
Poor - Just being honest. Of course there are millions of music listeners, but getting them to buy *your* music isn't easy. Pro recording artists with millions of dollars in advertising money behind them still dominate the music industry, even online.

LIKELY EARNING POTENTIAL:
Poor - A successful online independent artist might make a few thousand dollars. I know many who've only made a few hundred.

But then again, who can put a price on a bucket list achievement? Earning potential moves up to "great" for someone whose goal is to just *finally* complete a music project. After that, you never know what could happen.

Of course there's always the chance you get discovered by a major label, or your song goes YouTube viral and makes $250K like the girl that sung "It's Friday, Friday." But for every 1 person who gets lucky and does very well, at least 20,000 or more won't. *Becoming that **ONE** is the reason why many artists keep making music!*

INITIAL INVESTMENT:
Widely Varies - For one song, if you already have your own equipment, it's free.

If you have nothing, a decent DAW studio with a refurbished PC from Amazon would cost roughly $2k.

PROS:

- You finally got it done!
- It's a fun project to work on.
- You can quickly get your music for sale and streaming on Spotify, Itunes, Amazon Music, Youtube, etc.
- You can promo yourself for free on TikTok, FB, IG, Twitter, etc.
- Lastly, you could be that 1 in 20,000!

CONS:

- Most artists make only a few hundred bucks with their original song projects. If you spend thousands to produce your CD, you could lose money.
- It's very time consuming. Especially if you don't know how to use your equipment.
- It could be discouraging if:
a.) You're a great singer, but you make no money.
b.) You find out you're a terrible singer from your family and friends, but still make no money.

FINAL THOUGHTS:

I once made a music video with a friend. It took us a few weeks to film all over town. We didn't make much money from the video or song, but it was an amazing fun experience I will remember for the rest of my life.

If you need affordable mixing or mastering, I HIGHLY recommend my buddy John at JRmastering.com. John will do a great professional job for you. And if there are any major errors with your music, he will let you know about it.

If you need an entire song instrumental created, visit JaiMusicProductions.com. Just tell JAI the feel you're looking for in the music, maybe a few reference songs, and he will create a custom song for you.

I wish you the very best with your music career! Email me when you release your first song and I will buy it! **Pat@OppJunk**

10. Ebook Writer

This is similar to the previous section "Release Your Music CD." *"There's more to life than just making money."*

Writing your own ebook is a lifetime achievement I've heard *MANY* people talk about. One for over 40 years, and she regretted that she never got it finished. Unfortunately, now it's too late.

If this is *you*, **PLEASE GET STARTED AND GET IT FINISHED NOW!**

Get the book, "On Writing Well" if you need some pro writing tips, and get the writing software "Scrivener" which helps organize your entire book. Then set a side a few days a week to write 3-5 hours. That's how I do it. And if it takes you a year to write a 100 page book, who cares? **"All anyone cares about is the end result."** AND YOU DID IT!

Ok, back to the main topic. The biggest difference between writing ebooks and making music CDs is with ebooks it's *very feasible* you can earn a longterm passive income with them. Because, once you put your ebook on Amazon you just tapped into their free client base. You can also pay-per-click advertise on Amazon at a reasonable price. And the free Kindle Unlimited program pays for every page their several million subscribers read. Amazon is a great one stop promo place.

Comparing this to releasing your own CD, you simply don't have the same promotional options that an ebook has.

Note - Don't forget, you can also turn your ebook into a paperback, and an audio book, increasing your revenue streams.

BIZ MARKET:
Great - More people are reading fiction ebooks and trying to learn new skills since Covid dropped. And there are still so many great topics to write about, and wonderful stories to tell.

Even a played out topic like "weight loss," with millions of books written since Americans became fat in the 80s, a few people will make *a ton of money* this year with their weight loss and diet books.

I rank this biz as "great" because it's also passive income. That's a huge bonus. Ebook writing isn't going away any time soon.

LIKELY EARNING POTENTIAL:
Good - I've read online that most self published books sell under $500 a year, but I know some of these authors. All they do is write a book and list it on Amazon. They don't promote it, they have no reviews, and they don't advertise. They do *nothing*. Of course they're not going to make any money. In *any* business.

But if you create a few great books, self promote on social media, get reviews, and advertise a bit on Amazon, you can do very well.

INITIAL INVESTMENT:
Low - Everyone has a PC. I recommend Scrivener software for writing. You might need a cover designed, your ebook converted, and copyrighting, this will all cost roughly $150.

PROS:
- You have a great promo site available, Amazon.
- A good ebook is passive income that could last for 10 years per book, or even longer. With no overhead costs.
- Writing a book is a great lifetime achievement.
- You can write many ebooks and multiply your income.

CONS:
- Like all businesses, if you put nothing into promo (even if it's free promo), you won't sell anything.
- If you're just starting out, a 200+ page book will take you a *long* time to write. On the flip side, your second book will take you much less time.
- Some books you'll write, for whatever reason, won't sell very well. This is why you write *multiple* books.

FINAL THOUGHTS:

I wanted to mention this. There is an option for Amazon to print the paperback copies of your books, and mail them to your buyers. All you have to do is set it up on the KDP program. Note - A 200 page (8.5" x 11") book prints for around $4.

I've seen many book printers online charging $9 or more for this *exact same book,* and you'll have to continuously ship them to Amazon every couple of weeks as they sell. This is a *total* waste of money and time. Go with the Amazon KDP program and let them do everything for you.

9. Blogger Website

It's kind of like a YouTuber with typed words instead of videos. Starting your own blog still has many benefits.

I'm always asked, how do you make money with a blog? Here's the answer.

1. Affiliate Ads -

Amazon is the primary online affiliate paying around 3% for every sale, but there are many others. If you don't know what affiliate marketing is, first you sign up to become an affiliate. Then view what products you can offer on your blog. Each product will have a unique link that contains your account number (for tracking purposes). They might also have promotional pics or banners.

You then place a link or promotional material within your blog articles, and personally recommend the product or service. Any sales resulting from your website will yield a commission. Like I mentioned earlier, Amazon is roughly 3%. Some website offer 75%, or a cash bounty of $3, $20, $200 or more. I talk a little more about this in the *"Affiliate / Adsense Programs"* section of this book.

Note - Many times the super high commission deals are scams. For example, if you can get some fool to buy a worthless $5k work-from-home course, you get a $500 commission.

But then again, if you're that good a seller, just create a similar program (with some real value) and keep the entire $5k! Why give the scammer 90% of the profits and *you* are doing all the work?

2. Google Adsense or 3rd Party Ads -

Place Google ads in your blog articles and get paid every time someone clicks on one.

How much? This depends on the category your web page fits into, which coincides with how much advertisers are bidding per click. For example, if you wrote an article about music equipment, only a handful of advertisers (online music stores) are competing in this market. Not much competition means lower bids by the advertisers. You might get only 0.25-0.50 per click for these ads.

Now, if your topic is accident/lawsuit related, lawyers are paying $40 or more a click! But before you create a legal blog (which actually is a decent idea) Google will not fairly pay you for these clicks. You'll get more than 0.25 per click, but you won't get $10 per click either. My experience has been $2-$3 per click, though some claim $10. I've personally never seen it that high.

Note - If you're looking for *highest paying* categories/topics for your blog or YouTube channel, do some research and you'll find a lot of free websites that break it down for you. They'll explain exactly *which* categories/topics pay the most money per click. Then you can focus on these.

3. Sponsor Ads & 3rd Party Ads -

Sponsor Ads
A company pays you to sponsor their product/service in some way. A straight one-on-one advertising deal (no third party). It could be a banner ad, an article posting, or maybe a live video review.

Note - You do need a fair amount of traffic before a sponsor will even consider your website. If you're getting only 5,000 visitors a month, that won't be enough for most.

3rd Party Ads
There are several websites that offer to sell your unused website ad space for you, and then the money is split in some way.

I was looking for a few companies to list here, but the ones I dealt with several years ago are gone! Looks like there's a big turnover in this ad service market. There's a reason why all these companies are failing. If you decide to go this route, keep an eye out for any scammy behavior.

4. Your Secondary Products -

I saved the biggest one for last. Selling your own ebooks, courses, or even retail products is where you can make some good money. Do not limit yourself to ad sales! And you don't have to have an entire store. Just a few hot products to increase your cash flow.

BIZ MARKET:
Great - If there's an Internet, there will always be blogs and articles. And people who want to read them.

LIKELY EARNING POTENTIAL:
Unlimited - It's tough to give an average income on most of these businesses.

You basically have three classes of people.

1. The first group will make their blog site, put up five articles, and never visit the site ever again. They'll lose money from the web hosting and then close up in six months. I know at least ten people who did this. A few, I told them right off the bat if they were going to run their website like this, don't even make it. It's a waste of time.

2. The next group, will do a little more work posting an article a week and doing some research. But just the articles, that's it. No promo, ads or social media in any way.

"You can't even give away $100 bills if no one knows you're doing it!"

3. The final group, it's an article posted every morning, they have a fresh video every week and maybe a weekly (or daily) podcast.

There's a popular Internet guy in group #3 who swears by releasing a ton of content in all mediums. He makes over $120,000 *a month!* Granted he's been doing this for 8 years, he's living proof that hard work pays.

INITIAL INVESTMENT:
FREE - I assume you have a computer and the Internet.

PROS:

- Unlimited money potential, if you do it right.
- Passive income. Whatever you write will get traffic and produce income as long at it ranks well in the search engines.
- Writing articles is instant daily gratification, compared to writing an entire book that could take months, or even years.
- It's a home base where you can promote all of your social media sites and youtube videos (and then cross promote).
- You can sell your own products like courses, ebooks,and retail products from your blog.

CONS:

- I have to repeat, it takes time to build a great blog site or *any* great business, some more than others. You won't be rich at the end of this month, it takes time.
- Finding a great niche can be tough. I suggest a multi-niche site, to improve your odds of success.

FINAL THOUGHTS:

Like I mentioned in the "Pros," the blogger website nicely ties everything together. You can put your IG, FB, YouTube, and Twitter icons on your site and promote them all. Your YouTube videos and Podcasts can go on there too.

Get it going this week! Start out with an article a week. Then gradually build up to a few a week. We all have to start somewhere.

The guy who makes $120k a month, he didn't start out with 3,000 articles on his first day. He started out with ONE, just like you are. Actually, he didn't even blog or podcast for the first few years. He sold a single online course first, then he wrote *one* article.

Just get started on it! And email me when it's up so I can read your first article. **Pat@OppJunk.com**

8. Affiliate / Adsense Programs

This section explains the details on affiliate and adsense programs, so you can decide for yourself if either are right for you.

Adsense Program
Google runs an adverting program that allows you to post their ads on your website. Each time someone clicks on one of your ads you get a cash commission, 0.20 a click (which is what I usually get).

Commission amounts vary by genre, due to companies bidding against each other. A company promoting a $20 product might bid $1-$2 per click. An online casino or lawyer who makes a lot more per average sale might bid $30-$50 per click (crazy but true).

Obviously, the higher bid categories will pay you more if someone clicks on those ads. You'll get paid "more," but it's not an *exact* ratio. For example - Google won't pay 40x more per click even though they're taking in 40x more. You might get 5x more with the more lucrative categories.

FYI - There are other companies offering similar programs but their commissions are very weak.

Affiliate Programs
Many websites that sell products or offer a service, allow you to become their sales affiliate. How it works is you sign up for an affiliate account, put their promo link or banner on your website or social media account, and when someone clicks on it they are transported with a tracking code to the company's website. Anything the visitor purchases, you get a one time percentage of the entire sale. The percentage you get is outlined when you sign up. It could be from 3%-75%, or a flat cash bounty from $1 to $100 (or more) per sale.

For example, the Amazon affiliate program averages around a 3% commission (% varies by category). You could promote special deals, specific items, or just Amazon in general on your website. If someone clicks on one of your links and makes a $200 total purchase on Amazon, you get roughly a $6 commission. Even if you didn't promote what they purchased. I've promoted ebooks and the customer ended up buying a $1,800 computer. I made $54 commission on that sale, and I don't even promote computers. If someone buys a $200 gift card, you get commission on that sale too.

Also, check out Impact.com for a ton of affiliate programs.

BIZ MARKET:
Great - Affiliate marketing will always be around. There are hundreds of thousands of products and services you can promote to hundreds of millions of Internet users. It's all about the traffic you can bring into your websites and social media accounts.

LIKELY EARNING POTENTIAL:
Good - There are many people making $100k a year with affiliate programs and Adsense. But I don't rate this as "great" because it's highly unlikely you can achieve this in this environment. It's not the same anymore.

INITIAL INVESTMENT:
Low - Mainly just time.

PROS:
- No overhead, employees, and definitely no boss!
- You can quickly sign up with dozens of different quality affiliate programs in one day.
- Even if you don't make big money, it's another free passive income stream. It all adds up.
- A great addition to your pre-existing websites or social media accounts.

CONS:
- Some affiliates are scams, and won't pay you. Or should I say, won't log your true sales.
- With sites like Amazon offering only 3-4%, you need A LOT of sales to see some real money. To make only $1k a month you need $28,000 in Amazon sales. Don't quit your day job too soon.
- Google Adsense pays very low for most ads. 0.20 a click is not good.
- People are numb to Google Adsense ads (all banner ads in general). I purposely don't even look at them. This means low click through rates which equals low commissions. Note - You can still effectively sneak affiliate links within articles. This still works very well.

FINAL THOUGHTS:

Should You Get Into Either Of These?
Just starting out and going exclusively full time, definitely NO. Adding either of these to an existing site, definitely YES. And if you build a big enough following, *eventually* you could switch to full-time. But don't make that your *only* goal.

The PBN Networks

10 years ago, several marketers made millions of dollars with affiliate programs. They would create 500 plus boiler room (weak content) product review websites and link them all together.

Note - *Backlinks from other websites* was the top factor for ranking high in the Google search at the time. These marketers structured their backlinks so roughly 50 of these websites ranked very high, in the top five of Google search for thousands of product. This brought them in millions of dollars in commission fees.

This biz concept was great while it lasted. The problem is you can't do this any more. Google eventually caught on, and now does a "backlink website" search. Once they see a huge network of sites all cross linked together, they do a manual investigation. If the content is thin and the sites are primarily ads and affiliate links, they'll extremely lower the search rankings of all the sites in the group, which basically puts them out of business overnight.

So Why Not Make A Few Sites Using This Concept?

You can, and you will make *some* money, but it's not a good utilization of time. If you can bring thousands of people to your websites, you can make *much* more money **selling your own products yourself,** not someone else's. *Spend the time researching what to sell, and where to find it cheap.*

Here's the proof.

When I had my celebrity costume jewelry business, the site received 4,000 visitors a day (give or take 10%), every single day, 365. My sales were like clockwork, $350k-$400k a month. And my profit margin was 25% (not 3% like affiliates offer). In business this is considered a good profit margin, especially considering the fact that 75% of my biz was wholesale. And I had rent, employees, plus I did a lot of advertising.

Anyway, I sold the business in November, but the deal fell through. The next buyer wasn't taking over until January. I already liquidated all my stock and closed the business. But I still had control of the website for all of December. Here's what I did.

The web domain was still getting over 2,000 visitors a day for free (pretty much return visitors from over the years). So, I put the Google Adsense pay-per-click ads on the home page. The ads paid $1.25 a click commission. For the entire month of December, I made about $4,000 from the ads. That's from about 60,000 visitors.

Now you might say, $1,000 a week for doing nothing, I'll take it! True, that's not bad for doing nothing. But the last two Decembers my sales were $500,000 each. That's $125,000 profit. $4k vs $125k. That's a HUMOGOUS difference. Any way you slice it, selling my own products made *at the very least* 15x more money than the Adsense ads.

If You Are Honestly That Good At Marketing Promote Yourself!
As you can see from the example above, it's a waste of time to go all Adsense and make only $4k, when you can make $125k from the exact same website.

Now, I can see the argument. Who wants to mess with a dozen employees, a building, stock, etc. It's like being a baby sitter/high school teacher. Not like, IT IS!

But I would come back with, do it for two years and stuff $2 mill in your pockets. And then sell the business. Now you can do whatever you want.

It would take you 41 years to make $2 million if you're making only $4k a month. Do it in two years and get it over with!

Should You Get Into This At All?
Yes! I have affiliate links in all of my books, websites, video courses, YouTube videos, everywhere! And Google Adsense ads wherever I can put them.

But, you don't want to rely 100% on 3rd party ad marketing as your *only* source of income. They could ban your account and you're bankrupt overnight (this has happened to *many* people). If I delete all of my 3rd party ad programs right now, I'm still making good money.

Note - In 2021, Amazon started an affiliate coupon code program where companies offer a legit 25% (sometimes 75%) off on their products. You can post these "deals of the day" affiliate links on your facebook page, blogs, any social media or wherever you get traffic. These are very effective.

HERE'S A SCAM I FELL FOR

I wanted to mention an affiliate scam I fell for. It's either a scam or HIGHLY coincidental. No, it was a scam.

The scam company was an online music store. At the time, they offered 5% commission on all sales. I sent them 400-500 legit music related visitors per month for a full year. My commissions were like $5 one month, $8 the next. When I looked at my sales stats, they were so low it seemed like their program was broken.

At the end of the year I sent them 5,400 visitors and made only $60. I emailed the company and told them, "This is impossible!" I know my traffic wasn't humongous, but if only 1 out of 95 people spent $100 (some spend thousands in music gear) I make $300. And that's a low ball figure. But only $60? Not to mention if the company bought pay-per-click ads on Google it would have cost them $16,000. Why do that when they scam me and get the same traffic for only $60 a year...

I threatened to take the ads down. The affiliate manager tells me to leave them up, and if I didn't get $50 in sales this month (that's in one month), he will just add $50 to my account. So, I left them up.

Something strange happened. January I got $100 in affiliate commissions. That's odd. Remember, I got only $60 the whole prior year! February is tax return time, I made $300 that month. Miraculously, I went from $60 a year to $2,500, the year after I threatened the manager.

When the next year started, a friend of mine spent $1,000, but when I checked the stats it didn't show his purchase. Two weeks later I still never saw it. I emailed the company and asked what happened? I was told, "Oh,yeah I can see that $1,000 sale, we manually enter the affiliate commissions and we haven't gotten to it yet." After two weeks? Maybe you'll *never* get to it. SCAM!!

Needless to say, I deleted all affiliate links from this company. I was selling $50k a year in products for a measly $2.5k commission. The new manager tells me, "Well, we don't need you anyway." I replied, "Nah, your company doesn't need an extra $50k in sales every year." Stupid.

BTW, I moved everything to Amazon affiliate. I made a lot more money with them because people were also buying computers and gift cards. The music store didn't offer those items.

That's an affiliate scam. Manually entering in your commissions means they can *refrain* from entering them too. Like they did to me the first full year.

Valuable Tip - Before investing your valuable traffic and time on an affiliate program, have a friend make a very small test sale and see if commissions are in real-time. If it never shows up or is weeks late, don't waste your time with that company.

7. YouTuber

Everyone knows what YouTube is. But is becoming a YouTube broadcaster (YouTuber) the *best* money making option for you right now?

I've been following a fitness/life tips YouTuber for a while. After four years of making two videos a week (every week), he said his income finally reached $100k a year. But most of it wasn't from YouTube ad monetization, as you might think. Note - That year he had 250k subscribers and averaged 400k views per video.

40% of his income came from private Sponsor Ads (workout gear, supplements, etc.), 30% from Product Sales (ebooks & a video course), and only 30% came from YouTube ads shown during his videos.

This break down kind of makes sense. He posted 104 videos that year. If a sponsor gave him the reasonable amount of $400 to pitch their product in every video, that's the $40k right there.

As you can see, if he had to rely solely on YouTube ad monetization, he wouldn't be able to go full-time as a YouTuber, making only $25k a year.

Important note - His channel is in the health & fitness / self improvement category. Even though this is a good category, the YouTube ad monetization pay he receives will be lower than a YouTuber who focuses on, for example "making money." There *are* YouTubers in this "money" category making $100k a year *only* with ad monetization. On the flip side, if you have enough subscribers (over 1 million) you can make BIG money from *ANY* category.

My point, you have a better chance to succeed as a YouTuber if you don't rely solely on Youtube ad monetization.

Bonus Tip - If you *live stream* on YouTube, viewers can super chat tip you. I've seen many YouTubers with only 5-10k subs get a couple hundred bucks in an hour in super chat tips. Note - YouTube takes half of this money.

BIZ MARKET:
Great - Though there are many YouTubers, it's a fact that YouTube has very little competition in this market. Vimeo doesn't even come close in traffic numbers. Maybe TikTok, but that's it. YouTube will be strong for many years to come.

LIKELY EARNING POTENTIAL:
Great & *Terrible* - Thousands of YouTubers make over $100k a year. The earning potential is there if you have a great concept, can attract sponsors, and have secondary products to offer. And most of all, are willing to dedicate 30-50 hours a week. *Then* YouTube has *great* earning potential for you.

If you're going to post 1-2 videos a month, forget about it.

INITIAL INVESTMENT:
Low - If you already have a computer, a cellphone to record video and Internet access, that's free. Decent video editing software and a mic, add in $250.

PROS:
- Huge earning potential is there if you can make it happen.
- It's a great marketing tool for secondary products and businesses.
- Live streaming super chat is a fast way to make money for someone just starting out (once you pass the minimum subscriber threshold).
- Every video is passive income that can grab viewers *forever.*
- You always have a shot at that 5+ million views "viral video." *But not if you never upload any!*

CONS:
- *Most* YouTubers earn next to nothing.
- Creating an empire of products and sponsors in conjunction with YouTube content is a huge underrating for many. Some take this as a challenge they can conquer, while others take it as a reason to never get started... But remember, *you get what you give.*
- YouTube takes half of the super chat money.

FINAL THOUGHTS:

In 2022, I'm personally going to put a lot more time into my YouTube channels. I'm using them mainly as a marketing tool for my books, video courses, and websites. I might also get into live streaming Q&A's and tutorials for the super chat money. Creating a YouTube channel still has great value if you play it right.

6. Podcaster

Becoming a podcaster is like a YouTuber without the video. You need a good topic, you have to build a following, you can plug sponsors, some platforms provide ads, and it greatly benefits you if you have a secondary product you're pitching. For example, you sell your own ebook or e-course during the podcast.

BIZ MARKET:
Average - There are millions of podcast listeners, but this is *nothing* compared to YouTube watchers. But then again, there are far less *broadcasters* to compete with in the podcast market.

The podcast industry is growing year by year. Get in now and build your own niche before it's too late!

LIKELY EARNING POTENTIAL:
Widely Varies - If you build a huge following, you could make a ton of money promoting your own products or sponsoring 3rd party products. Or you could make nothing.

I guess you could say this about *any* business. What's your traffic, product/service and price? These variables greatly affect your earning potential.

INITIAL INVESTMENT:
Low - If you have a computer and Internet access, that part is free. A decent mic will cost you $50. Podcast hosting is roughly $20 a month, but there are free options too.

PROS:
- Free or low cost.
- Huge earning potential is possible if you can build a following.
- It's a great marketing tool for hot secondary products and other websites you own.
- Every podcast is a promo that can grab listeners and customers forever.
- Much much easier than making videos.

CONS:
- Many podcasters earn nothing. Especially if they're not that good, and don't have any other products to offer.
- Podcasting lacks the luck factor. There's no such thing as a "viral podcast." You *could* get 30-40k listeners in a month, but I've never heard of an unknown podcaster getting 5 million listeners in ONE DAY, like you can with YouTube.

FINAL THOUGHTS:

Here are a few of the main places to upload your podcasts. Buzzsprout (hosting), Itunes, TuneIn Radio, Soundcloud, Spotify, IHeart Radio.

The Internet really needs more great podcasters. This might be a great opportunity for you.

5. Virtual Classes

The difference between virtual classes and e-courses is virtual classes are live demonstrations, while e-courses are pre-recorded passive income videos. The live aspect of virtual classes brings you more close and personal to your viewers. Especially if you read comments and respond in real-time.

A few ideas - a live cooking class, weight training, stationary cycling (like Peleton), a cardio workout, motivation group, music (create/mix/master), dance class, computer repair class, appliance repair class.

News Break - While writing this book, I just saw a guy on the LA news who hosts a virtual cooking class. You buy a membership and he sends you a box of spices, ingredients like rice and corn, and digital recipes. You then watch his live virtual class and everyone cooks together. On the news story, 25 people were shown on his zoom screen. So, it *is* making money. Brilliant idea!

Google the term "Bollywood Kitchen" and check him out. Even if you're not into cooking or virtual classes, check out the layout of his website, and the professional look of his cooking kits. This is what I'm talking about when I mention making a big effort to excel in every area of your business.

BIZ MARKET:
Great - Covid keeping people in the house for months opened the door for this semi-ground floor opportunity. Now that many know what it's all about, this biz is here to stay.

LIKELY EARNING POTENTIAL:
Average - This is another one of those businesses where someone reading this will do everything right and make a few $100k, while others will put in very little effort and make nothing.

Whatever biz you decide to get into, *always go all out.* Strive for perfection! Give yourself a chance to succeed. And if it doesn't work out, try try again with something else.

INITIAL INVESTMENT:
Low - A decent web camera and maybe a few miscellaneous items. $250 out the door.

PROS:
- It's a fairly new ground floor opportunity. That's always where the big money is.
  - Another fun easy biz, if you have an entertaining spirit. A lot of people love to do this kind of stuff.

- Like any Internet business, your classes have worldwide access. You're not just limited to locals.

CONS:
- On the flip side, a lot of people HATE being in front of the camera. Especially if it's live. This might not be your cup of tea.
- Figuring out what you want to do that will actually make money. You want to get into a market where a large slice of the pie is still available, but then again you want it to be something you're knowledgeable in, or want to do.

FINAL THOUGHTS:

I saw dancer Debbie Allen on California local news. Because of Covid restrictions, her dance studio was shut down most of 2020. So, she went out on a limb and started an online virtual dance class. Her very first class on Instagram brought in 35,000 viewers from all over the world.

She didn't mention specifically how much cash is being made, but she charges only $5 for a single class, and $75 for a 24 class set (which is a great deal). And the number of streams that can be sold are unlimited, to some extent. All things considered, I wouldn't be surprised if she's making $250k a year with this, after all expenses are paid.

She offers 12 different styles of classes which includes ballet, latin fusion, hip hop, broadway, pilates, and zumba. If you'd like to see her website, Google search - "Debbie Allen Dance Academy."

Now, I understand Debbie Allen is a celebrity in the dance industry, and you're probably not a celebrity in any industry. But you can still make money if you're good, and market yourself well.

I know this guy who made and sold recording studio videos, but he never had any clients. He just passed on what he learned working on his own songs in his mom's basement. He was very personable, friendly, thorough and professional. He also produced a ton of free content. That was enough for him to be able to stuff a million in both back pockets!

Note - He got in this industry when the pie was uncut for a few years. When you have the whole pie to yourself, that helps a lot.

My main point, even an unknown with no credentials and a limited professional background can make a lot of money. It happens every day to *someone.* Why can't it be you?

There are a lot of virtual class ideas that are ground floor, or close to it. Now is the time in 2022 to stake your claim in this booming business, and make a name for yourself!

4. E-course Creation

E-courses are pre-recorded teaching sessions. Sometimes quizzes and printed material are included.

When the pandemic hit in 2020, e-course and ebook sales went up 25-50% across the board. For some even higher.

The leader in the e-course industry, MasterClass, ran commercials around the clock for months on several major networks. I personally saw their commercials 500+ times! This means their sales are up.

There are many e-course topics you can create. You can teach how to use any software program, music related courses, sports related, technology related, cooking, gardening, sewing, building/repair/handyman related, make a dating/relationship course (this one is HUGE), or maybe basic learning courses for children. See LearnBizOnline.com for more e-course ideas.

BIZ MARKET:
Great - Though competition is stiff, this is the best time ever to release an e-course since more people than ever are seeking them out.

LIKELY EARNING POTENTIAL:
Great - I know a few people personally who made over a million $$$ with their e-courses. It took them *several years* to create and market them, but they're millionaires.

INITIAL INVESTMENT:
Low - You might need a screen capture/video editing software like Camtasia, and a decent mic. $300 total. If you can't use your cellphone camera, make it another $250.

PROS:
- PASSIVE INCOME!

CONS:
- Making a video e-course is a long process, if you're new to it. A several hour course could take you 300 hours or more!
- Many topics are already saturated.

FINAL THOUGHTS:
I went the cheap route (no monthly fees) when selling my e-courses from my websites. It works well for me. I bought a Joomla membership software for $40 (onetime fee) and use Vimeo to stream the videos $84/year.

Teachable.com allows you to upload, stream and sell all your e-courses all in one place for only $29/month. This will work well for many of you.

You don't have to limit your e-courses to your own websites. Udemy is an additional place you can sell your e-courses. There's no monthly fee, but they do take commissions. You can even use Udemy exclusively to stream your e-courses (instead of your own site or teachable.com).

Udemy is similar to selling ebooks on Amazon. They take commissions, but they bring you free traffic. This might be a great spot for your e-courses.

3. Audio Book Narrator

I'm including this online biz because the audio book market is going up every year, and Covid lockdowns increased audio book sales by roughly 30% in 2021.

This job is self explanatory. You narrate audio books. ACX.com is the main website where people submit their audio books. These submissions appear on Amazon's Audible.com website, and are linked to the author's Amazon book listing page.

ACX.com also has the most audio book narrator job listings that you can apply for. Basically, you pick a project, and then read the sample page the author provides. If they like your one page sample read, they might hire you for the job.

Fiverr.com also allows you to promote your audio book narrator service for free. If you can read well, this could be a great opportunity for you.

BIZ MARKET:
Great (if the price is right) - There are a lot of audio books coming out in 2022, and beyond. There are also a lot of narrators available, cutting the pie up. What you charge can change your market potential from *terrible* to *great* if the price is right. I explain below.

LIKELY EARNING POTENTIAL:
Good - I did a lot of research trying to find an audio book narrator for my own books. For my 200 page book, on ACX.com, bottom of the barrel rookie narrator wants roughly $500. That comes out to about $30/hr. And most of these narrators I would consider at least one step *below* average in talent.

On Fiverr.com, anyone who has 3-5 audio book reads under their belt, they wanted $900-$1,200. Now that's up to $72/hr. Talent for this group overall was average, though some were pretty good.

Let's get to the point. If you charge $72/hr as an inexperienced audio book narrator, you'll be lucky if you get one job every few months. You might *never* get ANY!

If you're good, and you're willing to accept say $25/hr and undercut the ENTIRE audio book narrator market, you could get in a few narration jobs a week and stuff $4-5k a month into your pocket.

Now of course as you gain more experience and have more project samples, you can raise your prices. But never price yourself out of the market because you want to make the "big money" right off the bat. Always have income coming in, or use your free time on another project.

INITIAL INVESTMENT:
Low - A microphone for $50. You can record with free software, Audacity. You can also do all your editing using the free effects the Audacity software provides.

PROS:
- There's legit income potential here if you're good and are willing to start out at a lower rate. There aren't that many services online where the low bar is $30/hr, still make decent money with an undercut. Compare this to other industries on Fiverr.com like book cover design, logo creators, editors, ebook creators. The low bar here is $5-$7/hr. There's no under cutting opportunity here.
- Some people really LOVE reading. If that's you, why not get paid for it?
- You can split the work up and make your own hours.

CONS:
- People are picky and could reject the entire project, after you've finished. Or ask for a ton of re-reads. Note - I have no experience with this to say this is a common practice.
- You must deliver a complete audio book ready for commercial submission. Which means this job also requires editing out breaths, which you can noise gate out in seconds. Any mistakes must be corrected, and long pauses edited out.
- You have to have some talent in this area to be successful.

FINAL THOUGHTS:

Be sure your client listens to several pages of your narration, and they tell you if it's exactly what they want. Ask them if there's anything they don't like, so you can correct it before you get into reading hundreds of pages.

Also, a 50% non-refundable deposit should be collected (and explain it's non-refundable) if at all possible. This only applies if you're not working through a 3rd party website.

Listen to other successful pro audio book narrators. Get some practice time in. Checkout websites that have tips on becoming a great audio book narrator. If you really want to do this, you can! But you have to put the research and practice time in. Good luck!

2. Zoom / Online Streaming Buddy

Ok, this is a ground floor idea. I didn't even know what to call it. Win or lose, it won't cost you any money, just time. But it could be HUGE!

I saw an advertisement for a company hiring zoom Santa Clauses for $25 an hour. I went to the website and the basic package was $25 for Santa to talk to your child for 15 minutes. They had other packages that included more, but even the cheapest package the owner is making $75 an hour profit. Let's say he's running this x12 hrs a day, x5 Santas, x30 days = Over $135,000 a month!

Obviously this website is making AMAZING money, which is evident by the fact that their pay wage is good, and they were hiring eight Santas. They wouldn't be hiring them for nothing.

Now, I'm not saying to open a Santa zoom website, but the income this concept generates is *staggering*. It needs to be researched and expanded into different fields.

Note - When I mention "Zoom" I mean live streaming. I guess you could use Zoom, but there are many platforms. Some even let you charge a membership fee.
How about offering something similar like:

- Talk to the Easter bunny. This is very weak compared to Santa, but the pie is relatively uncut.
- Storytime for kids (StorytimeOnZoom.com is available as of Feb 2021).
- Sing-a-long for kids.
- Basic fun learning for kids.
- Live games for kids.
- Host a Zoom game show for adults or groups with prizes.
- Host a Zoom karaoke with prizes.
- General Zoom chat and companionship for lonely adults. I know this has been going on since the Internet was first created, and makes BILLIONS. But what I'm suggesting is friendly chat with your clothes staying on.
- Make a directory website that includes all of these, or offer several service options *yourself!* In Dec you're Santa, April the Easter Bunny, Jason for Halloween, etc.

Like I said, it's a ground floor idea that just might work. It's working beyond well for Santa.

News Alert - In December 2020, I saw a company on the LA News who started a zoom game show. The news story showed them doing zoom Christmas parties. They were going well.

BIZ MARKET:
Great - Because millions and millions of parents and adults were exposed to online Zoom learning for their kids, or Zoom meetings for themselves. Where will this all be in 4-5 years?

And NO, this doesn't mean every parent will hire a Zoom buddy for their child, but at least people "get it." That's the first step. They understand there are benefits to incorporating this type of learning once in a while.

Note - The Santa zoom has been around for years before Covid. This biz concept has *proven* it can be successful without a Covid lockdown. I believe others can too.

LIKELY EARNING POTENTIAL:
Great - If you get a good niche going and can expand it into several hourly employees, making a few thousand *A DAY* profit is *possible*.

INITIAL INVESTMENT:
Low - You might need to pay a small Zoom monthly fee, but there is a free version. Other sites charge $29+ a month. Maybe a PC cam for $50.

PROS:
- A true ground floor opportunity.
- HUGE earning potential.
- Low investment, low risk, high earning potential, and a relatively uncut pie. *This is my formula for success!*

CONS:
- It could take a while to really catch on, if at all.
- Once a company uses this idea and they publicly brag how successful and brilliant they are, there will be 200 pie cutters in six months. This happens in *all* businesses. Get in now and stuff your pockets before this happens! And please, *you* don't be the one to tell the world how much money this industry is making, and ruin it for everyone including yourself.

FINAL THOUGHTS:

It's interesting to see where this goes. If you start this Zoom buddy business in any market, email me so I can check it out. I wish you the very best of luck! **Pat@OppJunk.com**

1. Online Retail Store

Online retail is booming right now. If you read this entire book and don't know *which* business get into, online retail sales (even if it's only a few items) is the BEST business, for many reasons.

I sold replica celebrity costume jewelry for several years. Buy a ring for $5, sell it for $20, you profit $15. I was selling 2,000 rings a month from home making $30,000 profit, before moving to an office space. This biz was basically stuffing rings into envelopes. Beyond *super easy* money.

Compare this to, for example, opening a pizza business. If you sold 2,000 pizzas a month, you'd make roughly the same $30,000 gross income (before any expenses). But you'll need ovens, pizza makers (employees), someone to answer the phone, you'll have lease payments, insurance/workers comp, pots, pans, pizza boxes, and napkins, the list goes on forever! Not to mention when the 8-12 year economic collapse comes around, you're stuck with $50k+ in kitchen equipment, and a lease you can't get out of. *I'd rather stuff envelopes for $15 each!*

I'm just making a point that some businesses are much easier than others, and come with much less risk, and a higher earning potential.

Let's talk about risk. The example above uses a pizza biz making $30,000 a month. They were fortunate enough to be successful. If you were to start a business like this, there's at least a 65% chance it fails and you lose your $100k investment. I started my online retail business with $500 worth of rings. If I failed, the most I could lose is $500. But my upside was millions. And that's where the biz went.

And even if your income from an online retail business is slightly less than a pizza type business, the extra income isn't worth the headaches that come with it.

Also, online retail is worldwide with an unlimited uncapped potential customer base. With brick and mortar biz, the potential customer base is capped by driving distance.

Note - While writing this book, I saw an LA news story about people reselling expensive limited release designer tennis shoes. The biz is basically buy the shoes new for $400 and resell them for $4,000. This is possible because since the number of shoes released is limited, if someone wants them, they either have to either pay the inflated price or it's impossible to get them.

One major player said he made $600,000 the week everyone got their $1,200 stimulus check in 2020 (and he's been in the business only a few years). Many tennis shoe resellers claim they made hundreds of thousands of dollars, and they have the sports car photos on their instagram to prove it.

I'm not telling you "what" to sell, but if your goal is "pure cash" NOTHING BEATS RETAIL SALES!

BIZ MARKET:
Good - I'm giving this a good rating because even though Amazon/Walmart owns 3/4 of the online retail pie, and the rest is cut up into a million slices, there's a big increase in online buying, and it's only getting bigger.

Also, *you can* sell your products on Amazon too, in addition to your own website. "If you can't beat 'em, join 'em!"

Remember, it only takes *one* hot product to make some serious cash. Like the MyPillow guy. This guy made more money with *ONE pillow* than all the pizza places in NYC *combined* made last year.

LIKELY EARNING POTENTIAL:
Unlimited

INITIAL INVESTMENT:
Low - I started my costume jewelry biz with only $500 and sold over $13 million in three years. I already had a computer & printer, and made my own website for next to nothing. I know for a fact, if I did it, you can too!

PROS:
- Easy money with unlimited earning potential, if you can find a fresh hot product in a good niche market.
- "Online" retail means your products are available to the entire country (world).

CONS:

- It's a big pie cutter business. Once other retailers catch on to your "hot new products" hundreds will be selling them within six months, cutting the pie up into nothing.
- I've heard of some horror stories about brick and mortar stores moving over to Amazon online. Please look into this before you start.
- Huge money means employees and a lot of work. For those of you looking for passive income.

FINAL THOUGHTS:

Online retail businesses will continually experience profit pie cutting. But this isn't such a bad thing. In six month you can still stuff $100k plus in your pocket.

But you will always have to be on the lookout for hot new products. Don't fall into the trap of thinking your best selling items will sell like hotcakes forever. Prepare for an eventual sales collapse, and be ready to invest that $100k into the next big thing.

My Recommended Resources

If you're into music and want to learn how to mix or master, check out these other Opp Junk books written by John Rogers.

AudioMasteringSecrets.com
SongMixingSecrets.com
RecordingStudioSecrets.com

Thank You!

I would like to thank you for purchasing my book, your support is greatly appreciated!

If it helped you in any way, please leave an Amazon review with your thoughts. This allows me to write more books for you in the near future. In the meantime, check out my free articles on OppJunk.com.

From everyone who has been given much, much will be demanded; and from the one who has been entrusted with much, much more will be asked. (Luke 12:48)

If God put a dream in your heart, you have what it takes to achieve it. But it's up to *you* to put that dream into motion and make it happen. God can't move your arms and legs for you. Use the talents the Lord blessed you with.

I pray that the Lord blesses all of your business and personal endeavors.

Until next time...

Your Friend,

Pat Kennedy

PS - If you have any questions, want to tell me about your business, or need prayer for anything, email me at **Pat@OppJunk.com**.